BEYOND THE CLASSROOM

BEYOND THE CLASSROOM

Unconventional Education for a Changing World

AVERY NIGHTINGALE

Creative Quill Press

CONTENTS

CHAPTER 1

Introduction

Opening thoughts on the 21st-century school situation are offered in this chapter. As traditional education appears to be, qualitatively and quantitatively, on a downward slide, we are faced with questions of student disengagement, curriculum relevance, teacher burnout, and a school's ability to prepare students for the world that they will soon inhabit as adults. When the principles of unschooling, democratic schooling, and alternative education offer such promise, we must understand why these learning environments are not more prevalent, and why activities for bringing about progressive change are often requisitioned to enhance rather than replace existing educational institutions. A review of the author's thirty-year experience in the realm of educational alternatives is coupled with a sense of urgency to build a bridge between marginal educational endeavors and the establishment. As a dire global situation calls for a generation of solutionaries and leaders without bounds, grounded in an education without walls.

CHAPTER 2

The Need for Unconventional Education

One key area in which current education is not meeting the demands of society is in the understanding of the globalized world. Whilst international trade, global communications, and ease of travel are ever increasing, there remains a limited understanding of peoples and cultures outside the Western World. This is reflected in education with most secondary language programs focusing on the learning of the English language and providing little in the way of cultural education or studies about foreign societies. In addition to this, there are often xenophobic tendencies in Western societies with a fear and loathing of peoples from different cultural backgrounds, and this is often reflected in nationalistic educational curriculum with the teaching of history and the promotion of national heroes. With all the research done on the social harms of racism and the benefits of intercultural understanding, it can be seen that education is an area for considerable improvement in promoting a global community.

The last 50 years have seen great increases in technological capability, findings in science and technology, and the knowledge of man. However, these advances have not been without their resulting factors on every part of human life. Social and economic policy has often lagged behind in developing ideas, and application of new solutions is slow.

On the other hand, the speed of change in modern society, increases in information and communications technology are influencing how and where learning can take place. The result is an increasing incompatibility between the traditional education available and the skills and knowledge required to succeed in the 21st century.

2.1. Changing World Demands

Education continues to change with the times in response to the needs of the learners and the type of learning that is being demanded. The new trends are encoding the love of technology within our youth. This generation is no longer adept at functioning with only a pen and paper. With the increasing popularity of online education, it is imperative to provide access to information in a manner that is most familiar to the students. Simulation and "learn by doing" exercises are skills that are essential for independent knowledge acquisition and are in high demand from both students and industrial employers. On the same note, there is a high calling for more vocational and career-ready education. In the shadow of a recession, students want more "bang for their buck" out of education. They want to be learning applicable skills that directly translate into employment. Gone are the days of the renaissance intellectual. Now it is about being immediate and pragmatic in knowledge application.

Today's students carry a constant static of change in daily life. Globalization continues to increase, economies are in ever-fluctuating flux, and the explosion of information technology affects how we do just about everything. The education system, however, has yet to adjust to these changes. The traditional goal of maintaining social and economic stability has been displaced by a need for flexibility, preparing individuals to adapt to rapid economic change and to create their own jobs. In this new era, education and economic productivity have become inexorably linked to technology, making it mandatory for educators to prepare students with the skills and knowledge to function in a technological setting. In the new "information economy," the ability to work with and learn from information has become a primary source of creating economic prosperity. As teachers strive to provide students with an education that will serve them in the future, it is essential to remember that the future holds in store a very different world from the one we know today.

2.2. Limitations of Traditional Classroom Learning

Traditional education is oriented around conventional methods. This is a fundamental problem in a world that is anything but conventional. The term conventional puts forth the image of a process that has long been established and has shown a particular level of success. In mentioning the word conventional, it implies that anything taking a different path is doing so at its own risk. There are people in existence in the world today who learn everything they need to know while only attending the mandatory years of schooling from age six to sixteen. They then go on to live successful lives, learning what they need to survive by taking the easiest and most conventional path. This way of life was much less of a risk in the world that existed fifty years ago. In our world of change driven by technology and information, one must now take on a risk to follow a conventional path. An example of this truth lies in the dot-com boom of the late 1990s. The creation and success of many internet entrepreneurs, web developers, and computer programmers have painted a picture of success that involves little more than a pair of jeans, a t-shirt, and a lot of technical know-how. During this time, there are countless people who were/are well-educated, doing work that may not exist twenty years from now, in an office environment that will change over the years, and they will find a continuous need to educate themselves to maintain their work. This is a perfect example of change in the work environment that demands continual self-education.

CHAPTER 3

Benefits of Unconventional Education

The most important aspect of a person's time spent in school is the things that they learn and will continue to apply for the rest of their life. When knowledge is learned in a conventional school (reading, calculating, listening skills), it is usually forgotten very quickly because it does not stand out as something interesting, useful, and most of all, relevant to the student. The majority of conventional subjects do not stand out as something vital in everyday life. For example, "when am I going to use this in my everyday life?" The method of unschooling allows the students to learn what they want, when they want, and how they want. This makes the information learned much more clear and important because it was their own choice to learn it. The person learning is more likely to retain that information. An unschooler will learn in the andragogy style. This method of learning has 5 important aspects: a need to know, the learner must take full responsibility; orientation, learning must be problem-centered instead of content-centered; time perspective, the learning has immediate relevance, the learner and the facilitator evaluation. In this style of learning, information is retained for much longer because the effort put in by the learner was always in the interest of further understanding of the subject. With increased understanding, the relevance of what was learned is also very important because it helps the student's everyday life. This relevance causes information taught in the andragogy style to not be forgotten. This style of learning further proves that teaching does not always need a classroom. The information taught is from a facilitator and the effort is put in by the learner.

3.1. Real-World Application

"Jobless training" does not foster the attitudes and behaviors necessary for success in the workplace and community that students will encounter. By providing real-world education, we are giving students a chance to be successful and on our own with the safety net of good mentoring, constructive feedback, and assessment designed to help learn and improve. Combined with a good dose of reflection, real-world education can give students insights about themselves and their futures.

The importance of these real-world learning environments is that they allow students to test their skills and knowledge in a non-punitive environment. You can't fail if you never try, but students must take chances if they are going to learn and grow. If students are our future, we need them to rehearse for the roles we are asking them to play.

In a high-tech world with ever-changing boundaries, concepts, and behaviors, students demand more than ever that education should go beyond the classroom into the world at large. The worlds of internships, cooperative education, travel-learning, community service, and service learning are where students live education - not just hear about it.

Real-world Application

3.2. Critical Thinking Development

Lipman's Philosophy for Children program, Vygotsky's social constructivist theory, and Bloom's taxonomy of learning (which moves from knowledge through comprehension, application, analysis, and synthesis, to evaluation) all place a great emphasis on discussion and dialogue as a tool for improving thinking skills. It is suggested that high-order thinking emerges when there are shared thinking and guided interaction in thinking between individuals, focused on learning how to think and understanding content at a deeper level. High-order thinking is a greatly valued outcome for education which is relevant to students' lives outside of school when they are posed with difficult decisions. Cognitive apprenticeship where novice learners work in collaboration with expert problem solvers on a task has shown to be an effective way of developing high-order thinking. This can happen in the classroom setting and in the future has potential for providing a vast range of different learning partnerships and apprenticeships.

The more opportunities students have to practice constructing arguments and evaluating others, the better they become in thinking critically. Traditional lecture, essay, or multiple-choice exam format does little to develop these skills, but other forms of classroom participation such as role-playing, debates, or discussions can be effective. Dewey's claim that "when the method of the school takes the child's nature and the nature of things into account, the pupil's going out is a taking in the world in which he is growing" is a succinct summary of the nurture of critical thinking and reflective thought. The more we enable students to have hands-on experiences and think in terms of problem-solving and analysis, the more ready they will be to take on an active role in their world. In this way, there is a great deal of crossover between the development of critical thinking and the preparation of students for their futures.

3.3. Creativity Enhancement

It is a widely accepted concept that creativity is an exceptionally important human resource. It is what separates humans from the rest of the creatures on Earth, and in today's economy the innovative entre-preneur is highly sought after. The ability to think creatively is what separates good thinkers from great thinkers. In the future, it might very well separate world leaders from followers. It is an important character-istic that is not only taught at any level in today's school system, but may never directly taught at all. If there was any doubt about the value of creativity, the fact that the United States is currently outsourcing most of its routine "white-collar" jobs and employing more than 110,000 foreign workers in the IT industry should certainly make one think about the importance of teaching creativity as a 21st century survival skill.

The current American educational system does little to develop the creative capabilities of students. Just the opposite; as they progress through school, students tend to reduce their creativity in order to survive in the system. According to a study performed by KH Kim, a Professor of Creativity and Innovation at the College of William & Mary, on the creativity of children by age, 98% of Kong and Torrance's original sample scored at "genius" level. This is compared to 2% on a test of 200,000 adults. It seems the longer children go through the educational system, the less creative they become.

CHAPTER 4

Types of Unconventional Education

Project-based learning is an organized teaching method that encourages students to learn through active engagement in real-life projects. With project-based learning, students are not simply accumulating knowledge but are creating a learning experience for themselves and others (possibly an audience beyond the classroom), a development of knowledge and understanding around a central...

Experiential learning is an educational philosophy, which is categorized into four different steps: concrete learning, reflective observation, abstract conceptualization, and active experimentation. A very basic definition of this type of learning is learning from experience. It is quite easy to say that in many respects, experiential learning is what "real life" is all about. Often times, it is failure that leads our experiences, though this failure is not necessarily negative. Positive and negative experiences can be thought of as rewards and punishments for certain behaviors produced. The result of this experiential learning is the ability to make better decisions in the future, as the consequences or results of certain behaviors are able to be weighed more effectively. This philosophy can be carried out through a vast number of different activities and is not limited to any one type of alternative education.

Between the life directions of formal education systems, lie a number of different paths, often neglected, that offer increased autonomy and effectiveness. These paths lead in the direction of different types of unconventional educating. Four of these alternative educating methods are experiential learning, project-based learning, learning through on-line learning platforms, and apprenticeships and internships. Each of these methods deviates from the common memorization and regurgitation method of learning. They are also highly hands-on and contextual, directing students to take more responsibility for their own learning process, and typically more closely involve the communities and networks around them. All in all, they provide a much more relevant and meaningful education for today's and future generations.

4.1. Experiential Learning

Drawing on the fortuitous overlap between the students' personal, professional, and classroom lives, experiential learning utilizes real-life tasks and problems as the context for knowledge and skill acquisition. Learning from mistakes is neither a cliché nor an afterthought, but an intentional return to the work or task in order to understand and rectify one's errors. Experiential learning encourages students to take a level of personal responsibility for their own learning and to apply critical thinking in the construction of their knowledge. Its implicit values of democracy, social justice, and ecological sustainability are consistent with social work's traditional and contemporary missions. Experiential learning deliberately blurs the lines between the "learner" and the "teacher," positing that everyone in the learning community has the potential to teach and to learn from others. In an environment in which students are making, testing, and making sense of their knowledge, faculty become co-learners and more and more learning takes place between faculty and students. This is both a benefit and a challenge for many traditional educators; it highlights the changing roles of 'teacher as expert' and raises community learning issues at a time when there is a proliferation of individual and online education.

Experiential learning is a powerful and proven approach to teaching and learning that is based on one incontrovertible reality: people learn best through experience. The kind of "do and learn what works" style of education is what separates the MPH program from other Masters degree programs. This is more than an academic definition. It is a principle that underlies not only all teaching and learning at Antioch University New England but shapes the design, delivery, and evaluation of our academic programs. Developed systematically over the past three decades, experiential learning has been instrumental in establishing AUNE as a leader in progressive, higher education.

4.2. Project-Based Learning

Projects are generally multifaceted tasks that produce many tangible results. More often than not, students working on a project will be required to share their findings with others. This creates a good opportunity for students to work on their public-speaking skills and gain confidence. They must also use a variety of resources, from interviewing a community member to searching the internet. This helps students develop organizational and research skills. Finally, projects almost always have a definitive end. This means that students are working towards producing something for an audience. This is an excellent way to keep students motivated during their learning process.

The project-based technique places less importance on traditional learning strategies and more reinforcement on guiding students through hands-on experiences that require applying learning to real-world challenges. With project-based learning, students are not simply handed knowledge, but rather, they are given the chance to practice applying skills in innovative ways. The belief that a skill or concept has little worth if it cannot be applied to a real situation is a central belief to advocates of PBL. A well-known example of project-based learning would be to instruct students to research the impact of global warming and to make a recommendation to the town council using data from the internet.

4.3. Online Learning Platforms

Historically, online learning has been seen as the poor cousin to conventional classroom learning. In the past, online learning has had a tendency to be vocational in nature. However, over the last decade, there has been an explosion in online courses from reputable providers and universities. There are several universities that operate entirely online, with the Open University as the prime UK example. Online learning has many advantages which have led to its increased popularity, particularly in the corporate world. Time and location are no longer barriers to learning, cost of travel and accommodation are eradicated, and most online courses allow the participant to learn at their own pace, pausing and rewinding material as necessary. With the advancements in technology and increase in globalization, it could be argued that online learning is the future of education.

4.4. Apprenticeships and Internships

On the other hand, the internship program is good for university students because they can deepen their understanding of their major by working in a company that is relevant to their major and learning from experts. It also adds experience, more connections or relationships, and insights about the world of work, which is useful when they are about to step into the work world. However, they need to be careful in choosing the internship program. It should be paid and have a clear job description because nowadays a lot of companies use interns as free employees to do the dirty work.

In apprenticeship and internship, the learner doesn't just sit and listen or just observe, but tries the new skills in a real setting. The apprentice needs to apply what they are learning directly, and it can be more effective than classroom-based learning. It can also be said that apprenticeship and internship are learning experiences that focus on students working under the guidance of professionals. They will deepen their understanding of what they learn in the classroom. On the other side, the company will feel helped with the presence of an apprentice or intern. They can assign tasks that would be too expensive for current employees to perform or have the regular tasks done to free an employee to do more complex projects. Through this, the apprentice can learn a lot from real cases that they didn't encounter in the classroom, and the company doesn't lose anything because the apprentice or intern generally works for knowledge or a small salary. It is a win-win solution. This model is highly recommended for vocational high school or polytechnic students since the apprentice can directly apply what they learn in school, and they would probably be hired by the company because the company feels helped and comfortable working with and teaching a fresh graduate who has a low understanding of the actual job.

CHAPTER 5

Case Studies

By providing examples ranging from simple to complex, the teacher would be equipping the student with skills for solving problems in the future. But if the student cannot see the connection between the example and the general principle involved or if he has not realized that there is a general principle to be found, he might learn the details of this particular example or method of approach and it might stick in his memory, but it will be rote learned without understanding and will swiftly be forgotten if a sufficient amount of practice of the method is not undertaken to fix it in the memory. This is not a desirable learning outcome in law. Usually, the student is unable to understand the relevance of the given example to the understanding of a whole principle in a case example-based method. But if he is able to grasp this, he might later find it difficult to re-find the example in the case book if he has only a vague misunderstanding of the example and can merely recall the general principle or method associated with it. Finally, as has been described above, the student could fail to find an example of a principle and at the same time be unaware that he is missing understanding on a gap which might reveal the need for the knowledge of a principle. This latter example is of no use.

By contrast to the methods usually available in teaching institutions at the present time, for example expository teaching using argument and illustrative example, the student might be asked to discuss what would be a sensible step to take. This discourse now serves as a microcosm for the first method. But the quality of the teacher's questioning has to be more defined since he cannot allow the student to move stepwise through the whole problem since that would nullify the possibility of the student discovering a gap in his knowledge. The teacher would probably end up telling the student the suitable course of action and the reasons behind it – the example would have proved fruitless and a further example giving some simpler preparation for the first one would not be so helpful this time. High-quality questioning is a method of leading the student to the gap in his knowledge without statement.

The essential feature of the case study method is that the student is given a problem to solve, i.e. a task in preferably a 'real world' journalistically unstructured situation. In the course of trying to solve the problem, the student's understanding is gradually extended. He is driven to find information in his knowledge as it stands. Eventually, he discovers a gap in his knowledge. He becomes aware of what it is he does not understand. This interim of becoming aware that there is something you do not understand, which can be disconcerting and is usually avoided if possible, is the most significant learning phase in the whole exercise. The gap becomes a focus for a learning experience. This discovery, that certain knowledge is not understanding, is crucial. The teacher at this point can fill in the gap if exposition is to be the chosen method. But even then, the student may not be secure in his new knowledge. He has found out how fragile his understanding is. He will not fully believe that he has gained new knowledge until he has been able to test it.

5.1. Success Stories of Unconventional Education

With over two decades of inception, the ideals, philosophies, thoughts, and practices of Project Otenga and Rasta have evolved over time from sheer survival into a replicable model of affordability and sustainability that is rooted in social justice, ecological responsibility, and profound lengths of critical thought and analysis. By creating a holistic learning environment, rooted in practice and theory, we aim to give young Jamaicans a real alternative to the oppressive, Euro-centric, and morally bankrupt system of education inherited from colonialism. We value traditional forms of education that stress literacy, mathematics, and critical thinking. However, we do believe that the structure and content of education are ultimately informed by values, and the end product has as much to do with the process by which it is achieved as with the knowledge gained. Our goal is to facilitate learning that will empower our youth to take control of their destinies and become leaders and active participants in the struggle to make their world a better place. Through our efforts, we strive to provide a model of education that is relevant to the needs of young Jamaicans and that may inform wider debates on education and social change both in Jamaica and the wider world.

5.2. Impact on Career Growth

The idea that self-directed education can have far-ranging effects on the capability of a workforce to identify and solve complex problems is both intuitive and compelling, yet more difficult to measure. This anecdotal case provides a clear illustration of how a group of self-directed learners in a workplace used their intelligence, creativity, and communication and leadership skills to identify a complex problem and develop a unique, successful plan to solve that problem. In this case, the learners were a group of managers in a sales organization, and their identified problem was an underperforming sales department. Knowing that they lacked expertise in sales management but understanding that knowledge was preferable to ignorance, they decided to teach themselves the fundamentals of sales management with the eventual goal of using their new knowledge to improve the sales department and further their own careers.

The impact of unconventional education on an adult's career is inextricably tied to his newfound abilities, increased productivity, and job performance. In terms of individual career prospects, the logic is simple:

better, more highly skilled workers are more marketable, can command higher compensation, and have an easier time gaining employment, including employment with better benefits. Oftentimes, creative learners will directly apply knowledge or skills gained in their self-education to solve a specific problem encountered in their work. The capacity to instantly apply newly acquired knowledge to a work-related problem makes it much more likely that the individual will remember and be able to utilize the new knowledge at a later time. As new knowledge accumulates, it fosters the development of new, marketable skills that can be used to distinguish the individual from others in his field. This has the net effect of giving self-educated individuals increased confidence in their abilities and an enhanced sense of control over their own destinies, which has been shown to positively impact job performance and satisfaction.

CHAPTER 6

Challenges and Solutions

Lack of structure: To some, the nature of alternative education is perceived to be chaotic and unorganized. Practically, this may be true in some instances. However, these settings are breeding grounds for developing analytical and critical thinking skills. Acting on the notion that complex systems are, in fact, the summation of many simple systems, and if one is to affect change, it is best to work at the base level. Various projects initiated by students and teachers are testimonies to the creative problem-solving skills and the ability to act rather than simply talk - skills often neglected in students at traditional schools. These projects require the sourcing and managing of information from a wide array of sources and teach strong organizational skills and time management. Diplomas and certificates obtained through these endeavors hold no less ground than those from regular schools, as the projects often involve working with and gaining assistance from local businesses and other institutions. The final product is something both the student and the source of assistance can be proud of. This is valuable experience many schools cannot offer.

6.1. Lack of Structure

If more schooling can be shown to be unnecessary for reaching the relevant goals, then it is not "wasted time", and can be substituted for when the need is greater. The problem may then be not one of effectiveness, but of proving through some standard or another, that the young person did learn what he was supposed to.

We have found from our own experience, as well as from observing other alternative learners of all ages, that given the freedom to pursue passions and work on projects in a supportive environment, people learn very quickly and effectively. Time and again we have seen unschooled teenagers decide to go to college, and within one or two years of taking the GED or SAT, place into and do well in courses at a level which they had not studied for. This should not be surprising; if a person is naturally curious and has strong intrinsic motivation, tasks like reading challenging material or practicing math to qualify for a desired job are not unpleasant chores, but interesting means to a desired end.

Lack of structure will doubtless remain a difficult problem in alternative learning environments. Without the rigid scheduling and annually standardized curricula of traditional schools, it is hard to ensure that students are learning all the necessary material in a timely fashion. This is one of the most common concerns of parents making the switch, and has been posed to us many times in our research. It reflects a deep cultural assumption that learning is unpleasant, and were it not for the artificial coercion of grading and tests, a person could go for long periods of time without accomplishing anything.

6.2. Evaluation and Accreditation

At present, higher education is evaluated almost entirely through prestigious degrees and administrative rankings. Money in the education system is directed toward resources and marketing schemes designed to recruit the most talented faculty and students through these measures. While the incentives of competition in higher education often lead to material progress and instructional quality, it does so only indirectly. As a result, a professor selling a valuable but 'tasteless' course, as opposed to something more popular, jeopardizes his own career and that of his students. There is no claim here that a student of a great yet conformist teacher has not received his money's worth, but the endeavor is to provide more legitimate and tangible educational choices. This requires an equally direct way of identifying and rewarding effective teaching and learning. Given the establishment and momentum of extremely diverse educational goals and paths, it is time to coincide this diversity with the true nature of education. To do so, a broad yet unified framework must be set, through which unique student development can be encouraged and assessed.

6.3. Access and Affordability

The question of educational accessibility is critical and contentious. Accessibility here primarily refers to the ability of any student to engage in an activity, i.e. the cost of an educational program. This is of crucial importance for those unserved by conventional education, such as developing nations, indigenous people, and the poor. It is also important for alternative students such as older adults, prisoners, and disabled students. If a price tag is too high, it means some students will be excluded even if they are willing and able to learn. The cost of traditional education is high and rising. Financial aid is increasingly loan-based and is sometimes difficult to obtain for unconventional students, as is discussed above in 6.2. At present there is little data on the cost of alternative education in general, less for specific programs, and virtually none for comparative cost-effectiveness measures. This in and of itself is a glaring disparity between conventional and alternative education. Assuming cost will always be a factor, it is important for educators in unconventional settings to research and employ the most cost-effective methods of instruction. This is in the best interest of both their students and themselves, as efficiency in learning maximizes the ratio of educational benefit to cost, thus justifying the expense. Primary and secondary education has moved toward the concept of "education for work", in which the ultimate purpose is to maximize long-term earning potential. This has led to a situation where education is seen as an investment, and if the return is not deemed worthwhile, funds will not be forthcoming. Alternative students often have great difficulty in justifying the cost of education, as it frequently does not result in better employment, and may in fact detract from it. Step one would be a change in public perception of education as strictly a means to a job, and step two would be providing clear evidence of the non-monetary benefits of the education to the student and the society.

CHAPTER 7

Implementing Unconventional Education

Because formal education systems are so massive and entrenched, the most obvious and simple way to implement non-conventional methods on a large scale is to integrate them into existing schools, using the existing curriculum. This can be a difficult process, and the likelihood of success varies greatly depending on the type and openness of the school and its faculty. In order for this kind of initiative to be successful, it is crucial that faculty are supportive and play a central role in decision-making. An example of this was seen in Mindanao, where teachers and school officials, frustrated by the lack of government support, sought to enhance the educative experience of indigenous youth through culturally specific and empowering curriculum. The move was a reaction against the destructive forces of mainstream education, where indigenous children were made to feel ashamed of their culture and heritage. The project's early and ongoing success is due to the commitment of the teachers and their innovative use of teaching materials, rather than a direct attempt to change the national curriculum.

Recent trends in education have shown the growing acceptance for non-conventional learning methods and an expansion in the range of places where education occurs. These trends are occurring worldwide and have been highlighted in this paper in several different locations, including the following: Kenyan schools and their international aid-funded initiatives (Section 2.1), indigenous rainforest communities in Ecuador (Section 5.1.1), rural development projects in Guatemala (Section 5.1.2), and native title-affected schools in Australia (Section 5.1.3). The increased openness of formal education systems to innovate and break from traditional models has thus created a range of opportunities for educators to implement non-conventional education, both within the system and on the communities' fringes.

7.1. Integrating Unconventional Methods in Schools

Education generally changes slowly, influenced mainly by academic work done in higher education and changes in professional practice. Even more so than with other innovative educational approaches, the key to seeing unconventional methods more widely implemented in K-12 education is to have a well-articulated theory of action, combined with a compelling demonstration that this approach works better than the current one. The goal is to create a demand for this different kind of learning, such that schools will seek out tools and approaches consistent with unconventional education. As work has shown, children possess a remarkable capacity for self-directed learning given the right tools, motivation, and guidance. By demonstrating the effectiveness of self-directed learning in small groups with technology and other resources, unconventional educators can create pressure for systemic change, as parents wonder why their children cannot have this kind of education at their current school. Where earlier education research has often been poorly communicated and not easily translated into practical action, a key to building this demand will be to make a strong case that unconventional methods can be pragmatically and cost-effectively implemented in real-world K-12 settings. Indeed, this new generation of education research can and should be a form of teacher professional development, showing them a better way to do their jobs. A quality professional development program might be the entry point for a given school or district, if the case can be made that the program will lead to systemic change, rather than being just another add-on.

7.2. Community-Based Learning Initiatives

Successful community involvement in education requires the establishment of genuine and reciprocal partnerships. The word partnership is crucial here. Many schools embark on community involvement initiatives, but how many involve the community in the planning and implementation of those initiatives? All too often, community involvement in education has translated into schools seeking resources from the community. This is not a partnership. A true partnership means that all those involved have a stake in the process and in the results. If our intention is to improve schooling by strengthening it with community resources, then we must be prepared to share the control of schooling with the community. This, of course, is a frightening prospect for many educators and policymakers, but the history of education tells us that top-down initiatives for school improvement have a poor record of success. If education is to be improved, it makes sense to involve those for whom the education is being improved. And let us not forget that the long-term goal of education is to prepare our children to participate in and improve a democratic society. What better lesson in the democratic process for our children than involving the community in the schooling enterprise in a meaningful way?

Involving the community in the education of children may seem like a simple and obvious idea, but it isn't necessarily a straightforward one. Community-based educational initiatives can take many different forms, ranging from in-school programs to involvement of community organizations in the shaping of education policy. The common element in all of them is the intention to strengthen schools by connecting them with local knowledge and resources. This can mean anything from involving local elders in school-based mentoring programs to educational partnerships with local industries. Community involvement in education is an opportunity for schools to enrich the learning process by utilizing the resources that the local area has to offer.

7.3. Government Support and Policies

Perhaps the most significant form of government support for alternative and community-based schooling in the United States has been the charter school movement. The concept of charter schools emerged in the late 1980s and early 1990s, gathering momentum as states passed charter school laws to gain access to federal funding and grants offered through the Charter Schools Program. Charter schools are publicly funded institutions that are not subject to all the rules, regulations, and statutes that apply to traditional public schools. In essence, charter schools are one example of privatization in the public sector, being given more autonomy in exchange for being held accountable for producing certain results outlined in a legal contract (or charter) negotiated with the "authorizer" -- usually a local school board or state education agency. Charter schools vary in terms of mission, traditionalism, methods, and student populations, but all are designed to provide innovative, collaborative, and accountable alternatives to the prevailing system. Today, over 40 states and the District of Columbia have charter school laws, and it is estimated that over 6,900 charter schools are serving more than 3.1 million students. While the charter school movement is not without controversy and has shown mixed results in terms of student success, it is still a major step forward in terms of providing educational diversity and opportunity.

Government support for unconventional methods has grown substantially in recent years. In the past, alternative schools have often struggled for survival, operating on shoestring budgets and fighting losing battles against local school boards. Today, alternative schools of all descriptions, including many private and parochial schools, are eligible to receive federally funded "impact aid" if they serve a significant percentage of students from a public school district. Governmental support has given increased legitimacy to alternative schooling, particularly in rural areas. During the 1970s and 1980s, several states, notably California, New York, and New Jersey, established funding mechanisms to support alternative schools and community-based programs. A few states have also implemented support mechanisms for "at-risk" youth and secondary school students.

CHAPTER 8

Future Trends in Unconventional Education

Technology also has the potential to radically change the way we measure and accredit learning. Traditional assessment methods may soon become a thing of the past. Glen O'Grady, of RMIT University's Teaching and Learning Group, envisages student 'e-portfolios' replacing the traditional resume. This would be a digitized collection of learning records and experiences that are maintained by the learner and may include strong evidence of attainment and capable of being presented to potential employers or used to gain credit into a higher level of learning. Similarly, he believes that electronic simulations and games could one day provide an alternative pathway for demonstrating capability in certain areas of study.

Technological advancements are certainly one of the most influential factors contributing to the future of unconventional education. The strengthening of distance learning, through the use of online lectures, video-conferencing, and collaboration through shared documents, will become more prevalent. Watch this space: as links between virtual and real-world interaction in education become ever more complex, immersive, and lucrative. The immersive potential of Second Life has already been discovered by a number of tertiary education institutions, who have created their own virtual campuses within the online world.

Students are able to interact with each other and with their professors in a far more interactive way, without ever having to leave the comfort of their own home.

8.1. Technological Advancements

Virtual reality: The next decade will see virtual reality become cheaper, more immersive, and more widely used. It is expected that within the next 20 years, virtual reality will be so immersive that it will be almost indistinguishable from the real world. This paves the way for many creative forms of education and simulation. Students of the future could walk around ancient Rome, perform chemistry experiments in a safe and controlled environment, and travel to other planets.

Virtual classrooms: Virtual classrooms are currently quite primitive. They are usually a separate webpage with a few links, a list of downloadable material, and a forum. In the future, lessons will be conducted in real-time with an interactive whiteboard, chat, and in some cases, voice communication. Teachers and students will be able to upload and manipulate material, and lessons will be archived. Students can attend these classes from the comfort of their own home or office, which will save a significant amount of travel time.

Connectivity: Despite the progress in internet access, you will still find many parts of the world that do not have internet connectivity. Some areas that do have connectivity suffer from frequent downtime and slow speeds. Within the next decade, we can expect to have global coverage of high-speed internet via fiber optic and satellites. In addition to this, wireless technology is expected to have increased range and become more reliable.

The future of education will continue to be technology-driven. Currently, however, the internet has many limitations, and these are expected to be solved in the next decade.

8.2. Personalized Learning

In a recent official blog, ISTE's chief innovation officer outlined her vision for the future of education. While neglecting to explicitly define personalized learning, she discussed the potential for ed tech to act as a catalyst for the redefinition of today's classrooms. Beyond simply enhancing current models of teaching and learning, the CIO suggested that ed tech has the capacity to make a radical change to education. As the future of education moves towards a more learner-centered environment with increases in student agency, the most likely education systems to follow will be personalized ones. This postulation is a common one when discussing the future of education and what it may look like. However, it is not clear to see how personalized learning may go from being a trendy educational catchphrase to a universal system of education.

Personalized learning is a generic term for a huge variety of educational programs which are aimed to improve the learning process by considering the individual student's needs, skills, goals, and preferences. Although teachers develop many of their own strategies to facilitate personalized learning, computerized adaptive learning experiences have been seen as an efficient way to automate personalized learning techniques.

8.3. Lifelong Learning

The concept of 'just-in-time' learning, where the student learns something just before it is needed, is vastly more efficient for an adult who has a specific information gap to fill than scheduled courses taken out of pure interest or, worse, necessity to maintain one's professional credentials. A major trend in adult education is the availability of courses and entire degrees offered from universities across the world. This is often in a flexible format, be it evening classes, distance education, or intense short courses, to suit the needs of the working adult. The internet is a natural medium for the delivery of such education, and with the increasing use of web-based collaborative tools, it is possible that adults in the future will learn and build knowledge in virtual teams solving real-world problems, mirroring the pedagogical practices outlined earlier for young students.

Linking back to the earlier discussion of epistemological shifts, the ideal of the student who is grounded in a fixed time and place in the educational system no longer holds. The upshot is that we should seek to provide a good education, not only for youth that is capable of serving them over their entire lifetimes, but we should also remember the educated adults who want to consider a career change, or those who after years in the workforce find themselves 'on the dole' searching for a new direction. Learning resources need to be available for these people at a time, place, and in a format that suits their needs. Lifelong learning, though not a new concept, is now both possible and essential. With the rate of change in modern society, it is argued that one must continually learn new knowledge and skills to keep up. This is extended not only to an individual's self-maintenance, but in a world of rapid change, unlearned knowledge becomes redundant very quickly.

CHAPTER 9

Conclusion

As important as computer skills are, the basics are the same. Information must be digested and absorbed, problems analyzed and solved, writing and critical skills honed. All the actions on the computer should be emphasizing and practicing these basics. Information technology serves as a great aid for these purposes. Computer simulation and modeling can be helpful for understanding complex systems and relations. These methods are proved to be effective if they can be learned on one's own. Independent learning can be most motivated when the students are being sent to do a project. In projects, doing the work and learning to do it are inextricably intertwined. Learning occurs at a high level, but it does not feel like learning; it is what Dewey calls learning "under conditions of worth".

These are the abilities that are going to count. Since resources are tight, we cannot just add courses in creativity, innovative thinking, and learning how to learn. Courses in marginal subjects will have to be dropped. Instead, the entire curriculum should be focusing on developing these abilities. This does not mean plunging into a fragmented "computer literacy" program.

Our traditional view of education, a college education leading to a stable middle-class life, is out of date. The world is changing too quickly. The need is not just for good jobs but for adaptable and resourceful men and women. The traditional education is lacking in the teaching of resourcefulness and in facing rapid changes. Today's students will be having not just one job but from 3 to 14 jobs according to a U.S. Department of Labor estimate. What will see them through will not so much be specific training for a specific job but the ability to develop new skills, to think creatively, and to keep on learning.